What this book c

This activity book is designed to support your child's learning and growth in many important areas. It focuses on nurturing their emotional intelligence, helping them understand and manage their feelings, develop empathy, and build healthy relationships. Through engaging and interactive activities, your child will explore a range of emotions, learn valuable coping strategies, and cultivate essential life skills. The incorporation of meaningful Bible verses adds a spiritual dimension, emphasizing values such as faith, gratitude, kindness, and self-reflection. By engaging in these activities, your child will deepen their self-awareness, enhance their emotional well-being, and strengthen their character. This book offers a wonderful opportunity for your child to learn, reflect, and connect with their emotions and faith, empowering them to navigate life's challenges with resilience, compassion, and a positive mindset. Embrace this journey of growth with your child as they develop important skills that will benefit them throughout their lives.

Let's go on an
adventure

Emotion Recognition

Can you name these emotions?

Hint: happy, proud, sad, mad, surprised, frustrated, confused, sick, excited, scared, disgust, love

Emotion Recognition

Happiness: Laughing and smiling while playing with friends at the park.

Can you think of something that makes you happy?

Psalm 144:15 - "Blessed are the people of whom this is true; blessed are the people whose God is the LORD."

Sadness: Crying when saying goodbye to a beloved toy or pet.

What is something that makes you sad?

Psalm 34:17-18 - "The righteous cry out, and the LORD hears them; he delivers them from all their troubles. The LORD is close to the brokenhearted and saves those who are crushed in spirit."

Emotion Recognition

Anger or mad: Stomping feet and yelling when unable to have a desired toy or treat.

When is a time that you felt angry?

James 1:19-20 - "My dear brothers and sisters, take note of this: Everyone should be quick to listen, slow to speak and slow to become angry, because human anger does not produce the righteousness that God desires."

Surprise: Gasping and widening eyes when receiving an unexpected gift.

Can you think of a time that you felt surprised?

Psalm 31:21 - "Praise be to the LORD, for he showed me the wonders of his love when I was in a city under siege."

Emotion Recognition

Fear or afraid or scared: Trembling and hugging a parent tightly when hearing a loud thunderstorm.

What is something you are afraid of?

Isaiah 41:10 - "So do not fear, for I am with you; do not be dismayed, for I am your God. I will strengthen you and help you; I will uphold you with my righteous right hand."

Excitement: Jumping up and down with a big grin when told about an upcoming fun outing.

When is a time you were excited?

Psalm 118:24 - "This is the day that the LORD has made; let us rejoice and be glad in it."

Emotion Recognition

Love: Giving a big hug and saying "I love you" to a family member or friend.

What is something or someone you love?

1 Corinthians 13:4-7 - "Love is patient, love is kind. It does not envy, it does not boast, it is not proud. It does not dishonor others, it is not self-seeking, it is not easily angered, it keeps no record of wrongs. Love does not delight in evil but rejoices with the truth. It always protects, always trusts, always hopes, always perseveres."

Disgust: Making a funny face and saying "Eww!" when tasting something they don't like.

What is something that disgusts you?

Psalm 101:3 - "I will not look with approval on anything that is vile. I hate what faithless people do; I will have no part in it."

Emotion Recognition

Frustration: Stomping feet and furrowing eyebrows when unable to solve a puzzle.

When is a time you felt frustrated?

Ephesians 4:26-27 - "In your anger do not sin: Do not let the sun go down while you are still angry, and do not give the devil a foothold."

Confusion: Scratching their head and asking questions when trying to understand a complex idea.

Can you think of something that confused you?

1 Corinthians 14:33 - "For God is not a God of disorder but of peace."

Emotion Recognition

Pride: Smiling and standing tall after completing a challenging task or accomplishing a goal.

Tell me about a time that you were proud of yourself.

Proverbs 11:2: "When pride comes, then comes disgrace, but with humility comes wisdom."

Embarrassment: Blushing and covering their face when they make a small mistake in front of others.

When is a time that you felt embarrased?

Psalm 25:3 - "No one who hopes in you will ever be put to shame, but shame will come on those who are treacherous without cause."

Emotion Recognition

1. **Jealousy:** Feeling sad and wanting a toy that another child is playing with.

   Do you ever feel jealous of your siblings or friends?

   James 3:14-15 - "But if you harbor bitter envy and selfish ambition in your hearts, do not boast about it or deny the truth. Such 'wisdom' does not come down from heaven but is earthly, unspiritual, demonic."

Nervousness: Fidgeting and biting nails before giving a speech or performing on stage.

Can you think of a time you were nervous?

Philippians 4:6-7 - "Do not be anxious about anything, but in every situation, by prayer and petition, with thanksgiving, present your requests to God. And the peace of God, which transcends all understanding, will guard your hearts and your minds in Christ Jesus."

Emotion Recognition

Contentment: Relaxing with a smile and sighing happily after a satisfying meal or activity.

When do you feel content?

Philippians 4:11 - "I am not saying this because I am in need, for I have learned to be content whatever the circumstances."

Curiosity: Wide-eyed and asking lots of questions when discovering something new or interesting.

Can you think of a time that you were curious about something?

Philippians 4:11 - "I am not saying this because I am in need, for I have learned to be content whatever the circumstances."

Emotion Recognition

Loneliness: Feeling sad and quiet when missing a friend who is not around.

When have you felt lonely?

Psalm 147:3: "He heals the brokenhearted and binds up their wounds."

Calmness: Taking deep breaths and feeling peaceful while listening to soft music or reading a book.

What is something you like to do to help you feel calm?

Psalm 46:10: "Be still, and know that I am God; I will be exalted among the nations, I will be exalted in the earth."

Emotion Recognition

Gratitude: Saying "Thank you" and feeling thankful after receiving a kind gesture or gift.

What is something you are thankful for?

1 Thessalonians 5:18: "Give thanks in all circumstances; for this is the will of God in Christ Jesus for you."

Hopefulness: Smiling and feeling optimistic about something good happening in the future.

What is something you are hopeful for?

Romans 15:13: "May the God of hope fill you with all joy and peace as you trust in him, so that you may overflow with hope by the power of the Holy Spirit."

Activity: Emotion Recognition

Connect the emotions that can look the same:

Can you think of any other emotions that may look similar?

Answers: happiness/excitement, sadness/lonliness, angry/frustration, fear/nervousness

Activity:
Self Regulation

Box Breathing:

Place your finger on the line and trace it as you take deep breaths in and deep breaths out.

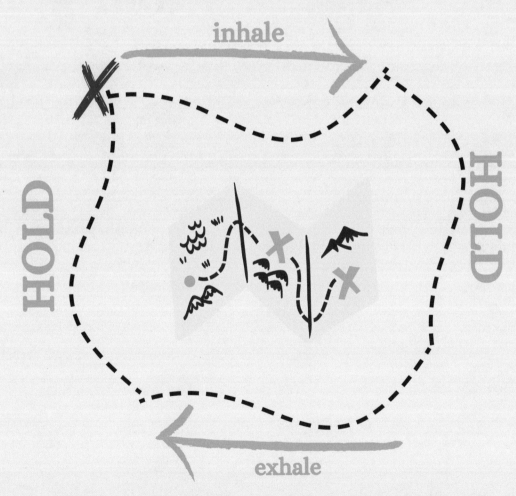

Repeat as many times as needed to feel calm.

Self Regulation

What helps you relax?
Pick a new technique each day and try it out!
When you are feeling frustrated or nervous, take some time to engage in one of these activities:

- Drawing
- Listening to music
- Hugging a stuffed animal
- Muscle relaxation: start from toes and work your way up your body relaxing each muscle
- Close your eyes and picture a calm place such as a picnic or beach
- Nature connection, observe nature by feeling textures or listening to sounds, going for a walk
- Yoga for kids

You can also explore creative ways to help relax as well. Find what works for you!

Galatians 5:22-23: "But the fruit of the Spirit is love, joy, peace, forbearance, kindness, goodness, faithfulness, gentleness and self-control. Against such things there is no law."

Self Regulation

Lets Practice!

Emotion | what you did:

Emotion | what you did:

Use a highlighter and highlight the boxes
that the calming technique you used
worked!

Self Regulation

Lets Practice! (scan a copy of this page to reuse if needed)

Emotion | what you did: **Emotion | what you did:**

Use a highlighter and highlight the boxes that the calming technique you used worked!

Kindness and Empathy

Ephesians 4:32: "Be kind and compassionate to one another, forgiving each other, just as in Christ God forgave you."

Draw a picture of being kind:

Kindness and Empathy

Real stories of acts of Kindness:
Take some time with each scenario to discuss feelings thorughout the story

1. Helping a Stranger: A child witnessed a person struggling to carry heavy grocery bags. Without hesitation, the child offered to help carry the bags to the person's car, spreading a smile and gratitude.

2. Caring for Animals: A child noticed a stray cat in their neighborhood and decided to provide food, water, and a comfortable shelter for the cat. The child's act of kindness helped ensure the cat's well-being and showed compassion towards animals in need.

3. Supporting a Friend: A child noticed their friend feeling sad at school. They approached their friend, listened attentively to their concerns, and offered words of encouragement. The simple act of being there for a friend made a positive impact and showed empathy.

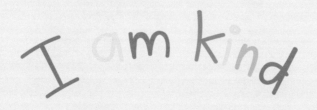

I am kind

Kindness and Empathy

Real stories of acts of Kindness:
Take some time with each scenario to discuss feelings thorughout the story

1. **Sharing Toys:** During a playdate, a child willingly shared their favorite toys with a new friend who didn't have many toys of their own. The act of sharing brought joy and friendship to both children, fostering a sense of generosity and inclusivity.

2. **Helping the Elderly:** A child saw an elderly neighbor struggling to carry heavy bags of groceries into their house. The child approached the neighbor and offered assistance, carrying the bags inside with a smile. The act of kindness demonstrated respect and caring towards the elderly.

Kindness and Empathy

Game Time: Emotion Charades

This activity engages children in a fun and interactive way, helping them develop their empathy skills by recognizing and understanding different emotions. By discussing emotions and their characteristics, children can deepen their awareness of others' feelings and become more compassionate individuals.

Materials needed:
1. Emotion cards (index cards or small pieces of paper)
2. Bowl or container

Instructions:
1. Prepare emotion cards by writing down various emotions on separate cards, such as happy, sad, angry, surprised, scared, etc.
2. Gather the children in a circle or sit together in a comfortable space.
3. Explain to the children that you will be playing a game called "Emotion Charades" to help them recognize and understand different emotions.
4. Demonstrate the game by picking a card from the bowl without showing it to anyone.
5. Without using any words, act out the emotion written on the card through facial expressions, body language, and gestures.
6. Encourage the children to observe your actions and guess the emotion you are portraying.
7. After a child correctly guesses the emotion, discuss the characteristics and signs of that particular emotion. Ask questions like, "What do you notice about the person's face and body when they feel this emotion?" or "What situations might make someone feel this way?"
8. Repeat the game, allowing each child to take turns picking an emotion card and acting it out while others guess.
9. As the game progresses, encourage the children to pay attention to the emotions of others and discuss how they can identify those emotions in real-life situations.
10. After the game, gather the children for a reflection and discussion. Ask questions like, "How did it feel to act out different emotions?", "Did you find it challenging or easy to guess the emotions?", and "How can we use this activity to better understand and show empathy towards others in our daily lives?"

Emotion Expression

By providing a range of healthy outlets for emotional expression, children can develop emotional intelligence, self-awareness, and learn effective ways to manage and express their feelings in a positive and constructive manner.

1. Talking or Communicating: Encouraging children to express their feelings through words, whether by talking to a trusted adult, sharing with friends, or even writing in a journal.

2. Artistic Expression: Providing opportunities for children to express their emotions through art, such as drawing, painting, or creating crafts that reflect their feelings.

3. Physical Activity: Engaging in physical activities like running, jumping, dancing, or playing sports to release pent-up energy and promote emotional well-being.

4. Deep Breathing or Mindfulness: Teaching children simple breathing exercises or mindfulness techniques to help them calm down, relax, and manage their emotions.

5. Play and Imaginative Expression: Allowing children to use imaginative play, role-playing, or storytelling to act out and express their emotions in a safe and creative way.

Emotion Expression

By providing a range of healthy outlets for emotional expression, children can develop emotional intelligence, self-awareness, and learn effective ways to manage and express their feelings in a positive and constructive manner.

1. Music and Movement: Encouraging children to listen to music, sing, or dance as a way to express and release their emotions through rhythm and movement.
2. Writing or Journaling: Providing children with a personal journal or notebook where they can write or draw their thoughts and emotions freely.
3. Social Support: Encouraging children to seek support from trusted friends, family members, or mentors who can offer comfort, advice, and a listening ear when needed.
4. Problem-Solving and Conflict Resolution: Teaching children healthy ways to express and work through conflicts, helping them develop skills in problem-solving, negotiation, and compromise.
5. Seeking Help: Assuring children that it is okay to ask for help when they need it, whether from a parent, teacher, or counselor, to navigate and understand their emotions in a healthy manner.

Ephesians 4:26: "In your anger do not sin": Do not let the sun go down while you are still angry."

Conflict Resolution

3 Key steps to resolve conflict:

Compromise

Take turns

Use kind words

Conflict Resolution

Complete the maze, when you come to an X, stop and state a step to resolve a conflict.

Matthew 5:9: "Blessed are the peacemakers, for they will be called children of God."

Problem Solving

Walk through each scenario, discuss possible solutions, and what outcomes may look like.

Scenario 1:

Problem: The child's favorite toy is missing. Possible Solutions:
1. Look for the toy in all the usual places, such as the bedroom or play area.
2. Ask family members or friends if they have seen the toy.
3. Create posters or signs with a picture of the toy to ask for help in finding it.

Scenario 2:

Problem: The child's friend at school is feeling sad. Possible Solutions:
1. Ask the friend what's wrong and offer a listening ear.
2. Offer a comforting gesture, such as giving a hug or drawing them a picture.
3. Suggest playing a fun game or activity together to cheer them up.

Scenario 3:

Problem: The child is having trouble tying their shoelaces. Possible Solutions:
1. Ask a parent, teacher, or older sibling for help and guidance.
2. Practice tying shoelaces with a shoelace board or a toy with laces.
3. Use alternative options like Velcro shoes or slip-on shoes until they are ready to learn to tie laces.

Problem Solving

Walk through each scenario, discuss possible solutions, and what outcomes may look like.

Scenario 4:

Problem: The child wants to help with chores but doesn't know how.

Possible Solutions:

1. Ask a parent or guardian for a list of age-appropriate chores they can help with.
2. Offer to assist with tasks like setting the table, picking up toys, or folding clothes.
3. Find a video or book that teaches children how to do specific chores.

Scenario 5:

Problem: The child is feeling scared of the dark at bedtime. Possible Solutions:

1. Use a nightlight or leave the bedroom door slightly open for a soft light source.
2. Create a bedtime routine with comforting activities, like reading a favorite book or listening to calming music.
3. Provide a stuffed animal or blanket for added comfort and security.

Scenario 6:

Problem: The child is having difficulty sharing toys with a sibling or friend.

Possible Solutions:

1. Encourage turn-taking, where each person gets a chance to play with the toy.
2. Suggest playing a game together that requires sharing, like building with blocks or playing catch.
3. Set a timer for each child's designated playtime with the toy to ensure fairness

Problem Solving

Walk through each scenario, discuss possible solutions, and what outcomes may look like.

Scenario 7:

Problem: The child accidentally spills their drink at the dinner table.

Possible Solutions:

1. Quickly grab a towel or napkin to soak up the spill and prevent it from spreading.
2. Apologize to parents or guardians for the accident and offer to help clean up.
3. Learn to be more cautious by holding cups with both hands or using spill-proof containers.

Scenario 8:

Problem: The child is feeling bored during a long car ride. Possible Solutions:

1. Play travel games like "I Spy," the license plate game, or counting different colored cars.
2. Bring along books, coloring books, or small toys to keep busy during the ride.
3. Listen to an audiobook or sing along to favorite songs to make the time more enjoyable.

Scenario 9:

Problem: The child has too many toys and can't keep them organized.

Possible Solutions:

1. Sort toys into different categories and designate specific storage bins or shelves for each category.
2. Donate or give away toys that are no longer played with or needed to make space for new ones.
3. Create a cleaning-up routine before bedtime or a specific time of the day to ensure toys are put away.

Problem Solving Conflicts

Walk through each scenario, discuss possible solutions, and what outcomes may look like.

Scenario 1:

Problem: The child and their friend both want to play with the same toy.
Possible Solutions:

1. Take turns playing with the toy, setting a timer for each turn.
2. Find another toy or game that both children can enjoy together.
3. Ask a grown-up or teacher to help mediate and find a fair solution.

Scenario 2:

Problem: The child's sibling accidentally breaks one of their favorite possessions. Possible Solutions:

1. Express their feelings to the sibling and explain why the possession is important to them.
2. Work together with the sibling to repair or fix the broken item, if possible.
3. Practice forgiveness and understanding that accidents happen, and belongings can be replaced.

Scenario 3:

Problem: The child's classmate is being unkind or mean to them. Possible Solutions:

1. Talk to the classmate about how their behavior is making the child feel and ask them to stop.
2. Seek help from a teacher or trusted adult to address the situation.
3. Surround themselves with supportive friends and engage in activities that make them feel good about themselves.

Problem Solving Conflicts

Walk through each scenario, discuss possible solutions, and what outcomes may look like.

Scenario 4:

Problem: The child and a friend want to play different games but can't agree on one. Possible Solutions:

1. Take turns playing each game for a designated period of time.
2. Find a compromise by choosing a game that combines elements from both preferred games.
3. Invite more friends to join and play different games simultaneously.

Scenario 5:

Problem: The child's classmate is being left out by other children during recess. Possible Solutions:

1. Include the classmate in their games and activities, making them feel welcomed and included.
2. Talk to other classmates about being kind and inclusive, encouraging them to invite the classmate to join.
3. Inform a teacher or recess monitor about the situation, so they can help ensure everyone is included.

Scenario 6:

Problem: The child and a friend disagree on which TV show or movie to watch. Possible Solutions:

1. Take turns choosing the show or movie on different days or occasions.
2. Find a show or movie that both friends are interested in and compromise on the choice.
3. Suggest watching one episode or part of each show or movie to cater to both preferences

Problem Solving Conflicts

Walk through each scenario, discuss possible solutions, and what outcomes may look like.

Scenario 7:

Problem: The child's friend accidentally takes their snack or lunchbox by mistake. Possible Solutions:

1. Politely inform the friend about the mix-up and ask for their snack or lunchbox back.
2. Offer to share the snack or lunch until the friend can get their own.
3. Label the child's belongings with their name to avoid future mix-ups.

Scenario 8:

Problem: The child and their sibling have a disagreement over what game to play together. Possible Solutions:

1. Take turns playing each other's preferred games for a specific amount of time.
2. Find a game that combines elements from both preferences or create a new game together.
3. Involve a parent or guardian to help mediate and find a fair solution.

Scenario 9:

Problem: The child and a friend have a disagreement about the rules of a game they are playing. Possible Solutions:

1. Discuss and negotiate the rules with the friend, finding a compromise that works for both.
2. Look up the official rules of the game online or in a rulebook to resolve the disagreement.
3. Take a break from the game, play something else together, and revisit the game later with a fresh perspective.

Problem Solving Conflicts

Can you think of times when you faced a problem and you were unsure how to solve the problem or conflict?

Reflect on this time, what could have been done?

How does God want us to handle conflict and problems?

Proverbs 3:5-6: "Trust in the LORD with all your heart and lean not on your own understanding; in all your ways submit to him, and he will make your paths straight."

This verse reminds us to rely on God for guidance and wisdom in problem-solving. It encourages us to trust in God's understanding and submit our ways to Him. By seeking His direction and following His guidance, we can navigate through challenges and find clarity in our decision-making processes.

Gratitude

What are you thankful for?

_____

_____

_____

_____

_____

_____

_____

_____

1 Thessalonians 5:18: "Give thanks in all circumstances; for this is God's will for you in Christ Jesus."

This verse emphasizes the importance of gratitude in all aspects of life. It encourages us to have a thankful heart regardless of our circumstances. By expressing gratitude, we align ourselves with God's will and cultivate a positive and appreciative attitude towards the blessings we receive.

Gratitude

How to incorporate every day:

1. Provide them with a notebook or sheets of paper and writing utensils.
2. Encourage the child to set aside a few minutes each day to reflect on and write down things they are grateful for.
3. Guide them to think about different aspects of their life, such as family, friends, activities, nature, talents, or experiences.
4. Each day, have the child write down at least three things they are grateful for. These can be big or small things.
5. Encourage them to be specific and descriptive in their entries, explaining why they are grateful for each item or experience.
6. Emphasize that the journal is personal and private, allowing the child to freely express their thoughts and feelings.
7. Encourage them to decorate the journal or add drawings alongside their gratitude entries if they wish.
8. Set a regular time for the child to engage in this activity, such as before bed or during a quiet moment in the day.
9. As an optional extension, you can encourage them to share their gratitude reflections with a family member or discuss them during a family conversation time.

By engaging in this activity regularly, children can develop a habit of recognizing and appreciating the positive aspects of their lives. It helps cultivate a mindset of gratitude and fosters a sense of contentment and happiness.

Positive Thinking

Encourage your child to say 1 these affirmations aloud or write them down daily. Remind them of their worth, abilities, and positive qualities, empowering them to believe in themselves and embrace their unique potential.

1. I am loved and cared for.
2. I am strong and capable.
3. I have a unique and special purpose in this world.
4. I am smart and have the ability to learn new things.
5. I am kind and treat others with respect.
6. I am brave and can face challenges with courage.
7. I am creative and have a wonderful imagination.
8. I am important and my thoughts and feelings matter.
9. I am surrounded by people who believe in me.
10. I am responsible and can make good choices.
11. I am deserving of happiness and success.
12. I am resilient and can bounce back from tough times.
13. I am worthy of love and affection.

1. I am a good friend and bring joy to others.
2. I am patient and can wait for good things to come.
3. I am generous and enjoy sharing with others.
4. I am beautiful/handsome both inside and out.
5. I am loved for who I am, just as I am.
6. I am capable of achieving my goals and dreams.
7. I am grateful for the blessings in my life.
8. I am deserving of forgiveness and can forgive others.
9. I am helpful and make a positive difference in the world.
10. I am full of potential and have endless possibilities.
11. I am loved unconditionally by my family and friends.
12. I am enough, just the way I am.

Activity:
Coping Collage

Materials:
Magazines
Scissors
Glue
Large paper or cardboard/poster board

Instructions:
- Have your child/children to search for images that represent different coping strategies, such as deep breathing, talking to a friend, engaging in a hobby, or going for a walk.
- Have them cut out the images and glue them onto the paper to create a collage of coping strategies.
- Encourage them to discuss each strategy and how they can use it when faced with challenging situations.

Activity:
Emotion Reflection Art

Materials:
variety of art supplies

Instructions:
- Instruct children to create artwork that represents a specific emotion or a mix of emotions.
- After completing their artwork, encourage them to reflect on the process and discuss the emotions they aimed to convey.

Activity: Emotion Dance Party

Instructions:

- Create a playlist of songs that evoke different emotions, such as happiness, sadness, excitement, and calmness.
- Encourage children to dance freely, expressing the emotions they feel while listening to each song.
- After the dance party, discuss the emotions experienced during different songs and how movement can help express and regulate emotions.

Activity:
Emotion and Bible Verse Reflection

Instructions:

- Select a Bible verse that relates to emotions (can use one provided in this book, or a different verse)
- read it through a couple of times
- write down reflections on how your child can apply its message to manage emotions in various situations
- encourage regular journaling incorporating different bible verses that speak different messages and coping strategies

_____

_____

_____

_____

_____

_____

_____

_____

_____

_____

_____

_____

_____

Activity:
Emotion and Bible Verse Reflection

Additional Pages:
Iff this activity is enojyed, I reccomend getting a jou

_____

_____

_____

_____

_____

_____

_____

_____

_____

_____

_____

_____

Activity:
Emotion and Bible Verse Reflection

Additional Pages:
Iff this activity is enojyed, I reccomend getting a jou

_____

_____

_____

_____

_____

_____

_____

_____

_____

_____

_____

_____

_____

_____

Confidence

Confidence is believing in yourself and your abilities. It means knowing that you have unique qualities and strengths that make you special. When you have confidence, you feel sure of yourself and your capabilities. It's important to remember that everyone has moments of doubt or insecurity, but having confidence helps us overcome those feelings and keep moving forward. Building confidence takes practice and positive thinking. Focus on your strengths, set goals for yourself, and celebrate your achievements, No matter how big or small. Remember, you are capable of amazing things, and with a little belief in yourself, you can accomplish anything you set your mind to.

Philippians 4:13: "I can do all things through Christ who strengthens me."

This Bible verse from Philippians emphasizes the confidence that comes from relying on God's strength. It reminds us that with God's help, we can face challenges and accomplish great things. It instills a sense of assurance and belief in our abilities, knowing that we are not alone and can draw upon the power of Christ to overcome obstacles and pursue our goals with confidence.

Activity: Confidence

Materials needed:

- Mirror
- Index cards or small pieces of paper
- Writing utensils

Instructions:

1. Begin by discussing with the child what confidence means and why it is important.
2. Set up a comfortable space with a mirror placed at a suitable height for the child.
3. Ask the child to stand in front of the mirror and take a few moments to observe their reflection.
4. Explain that confidence comes from within and that they have unique qualities and strengths that make them special.
5. Provide the child with index cards or small pieces of paper.
6. Instruct them to write down positive affirmations or statements that reflect their strengths, abilities, and accomplishments.
7. Encourage them to think about what they like about themselves, their skills, or their achievements.
8. After writing the affirmations, ask the child to read them aloud while looking at themselves in the mirror.
9. Have them repeat the affirmations a few times, emphasizing the importance of believing in their own abilities and worth.
10. Engage in a discussion with the child, asking them how it feels to express positive affirmations and reflect on their strengths.
11. Encourage them to continue practicing this activity regularly, adding new affirmations or modifying existing ones as they grow in confidence.

Resilience

Scenarios:

1. A child is practicing riding a bike but keeps falling off.
   - Teach resilience: Encourage the child to keep trying and remind them that it's normal to make mistakes and experience setbacks when learning something new. Emphasize the importance of getting back on the bike, practicing, and celebrating small improvements along the way.

2. A child feels disappointed after not being chosen for a sports team or a school performance.
   - Teach resilience: Help the child understand that not being selected doesn't define their worth or abilities. Encourage them to focus on their strengths, explore other interests, and remind them that opportunities will come again. Discuss stories of famous athletes or performers who faced similar setbacks but persevered and succeeded.

3. A child is struggling with a challenging homework assignment or school project.
   - Teach resilience: Guide the child in breaking the task into smaller, manageable steps. Encourage them to ask for help, seek guidance from their teacher or classmates, and practice self-encouragement and positive self-talk. Emphasize the value of effort and persistence in overcoming challenges.

Resilience

Scenarios:

1. Scenario: A child experiences conflict with a friend or sibling.
   - Teach resilience: Help the child understand that conflicts are a normal part of relationships and provide opportunities for growth. Teach them conflict resolution strategies such as active listening, expressing feelings calmly, and finding compromises. Encourage them to view conflicts as opportunities to strengthen relationships and learn new ways of communicating.
2. Scenario: A child feels nervous or anxious before a school presentation or performance.
   - Teach resilience: Teach the child calming techniques such as deep breathing or visualization. Encourage them to practice and prepare for the event, emphasizing that nervousness is natural but can be managed. Remind them of past accomplishments and moments when they successfully faced similar challenges, building their confidence and resilience.

By presenting these scenarios and teaching resilience in age-appropriate ways, children can develop the mindset, skills, and strategies to navigate setbacks, challenges, and adversity with resilience and a positive outlook. Encourage open discussions, provide guidance and support, and reinforce the idea that resilience is an important life skill that can lead to personal growth and success. Another word for resilience is perseverance.

Romans 5:3-4: "Not only so, but we also glory in our sufferings, because we know that suffering produces perseverance; perseverance, character; and character, hope."

Self-Awareness

Teaching self-awareness to children involves helping them develop an understanding of their own thoughts, emotions, and behaviors. By engaging in activities that encourage reflection, exploration of emotions, and self-expression, children can cultivate a deeper sense of self, which leads to enhanced emotional intelligence, improved decision-making, and stronger interpersonal relationships.

Psalm 139:23-24: "Search me, God, and know my heart; test me and know my anxious thoughts. See if there is any offensive way in me, and lead me in the way everlasting."

This Bible verse from Psalm 139 expresses the desire for self-awareness and invites God to examine one's heart and thoughts. It reflects the importance of introspection and recognizing our own weaknesses or shortcomings. By seeking self-awareness with God's guidance, we can strive for personal growth and align ourselves with His everlasting ways.

Activity: Self-Awareness

Feelings Check-In:

- Have children sit in a circle or individually.
- Provide a list of different emotions and ask each child to choose and share an emotion they are currently experiencing.
- Encourage them to explain why they feel that way, helping them identify and articulate their emotions.

Activity: Self-Awareness

Mindful Moments:

- Lead children through a short mindfulness exercise, focusing their attention on their breath and the present moment.
- Encourage them to notice and describe how they are feeling physically, emotionally, and mentally during the exercise.
- Afterward, facilitate a discussion about their observations, helping them develop a deeper awareness of their internal state.

Activity: Self-Awareness

Self-Portrait:

- Provide art supplies such as paper, crayons, markers, and paints.
- Ask children to create a self-portrait, focusing on drawing themselves and their facial expressions.
- After completing the self-portrait, have a discussion about the emotions they depicted and why they chose to represent themselves in that way.

Activity:
Emotion Storytelling

- Ask children to create their own stories that revolve around different social-emotional themes, such as friendship, empathy, or kindness.
- They can either write the stories or orally share them with the group.
- After each story, facilitate a discussion about the social-emotional lessons learned and how the characters in the story displayed those skills.

Activity: Emotion Walk

- Create a designated space, indoors or outdoors, for an "emotion walk."
- Mark different areas with signs representing various emotions.
- Children walk around the space, and when they reach a specific emotion sign, they have to demonstrate the body language or facial expressions associated with that emotion.
- Encourage them to discuss how they recognize emotions in themselves and others.

LET'S GO

ADVENTURE

Activity:
Emotion Reflection Art

- Provide art supplies and ask children to create individual art pieces that express different emotions or social-emotional themes.
- Once completed, set up an "emotion reflection art gallery" where each child displays their artwork.
- Give them the opportunity to explain the emotions or themes represented in their art and engage in discussions about how those emotions impact social interactions and relationships.

Activity: Feelings Matching Game

Activity:
Feelings Matching Game

Remember, social-emotional learning is a continuous process, and it's important to provide ongoing opportunities for children to practice during real life situations and reinforce these skills. Incorporating these additional skills into your teaching or activities can further enhance their emotional intelligence, interpersonal skills, and overall well-being.